CW00407082

LEGENDS

BETHANY NOLAN

For myself, because I deserve it.

Also for my Grandad, Keith Nolan, who passed the writing gene down to me.

ACKNOWLEDGMENTS

When I was very young, I was on the beach, and my mother pointed to where I was supposed to go to join the main group by the water. Instead of going there, I walked in a different direction and ended up lost.
Thank you to the woman who found me, and helped me get back to my family.

Also to my parents, for not leaving me on that beach, to my friends, for teaching me rude words, and to Lana, for encouraging me to write this in the first place.

(Also, to Scamper, because you were just a really great rabbit.)

ACHILLES I

You must have loved him more than anything.
Maybe it wasn't your heel.
Maybe it was him.

ICARUS

did it hurt
to love something that you could never have

the sun, i mean

did it hurt to love something so much that you'd
let it kill you,
tell me,
i'd like to try it some time

and the water

was it cold on your skin
did it wash away your wings

i'm afraid to lose mine
i'm afraid to let the wax melt
i'd give you my wings if i could
if i knew you'd be careful with them

child, did it hurt when you fell
was the flight worth it

what was the last thing you saw
was it the sun
the water
the bronze feathers escaping you
one by one

or was it just the sky, clear and vast above you

did you scream

did it hurt

where did you go

i miss having someone to fly with

HYACINTHUS I

what is it like to be loved by the sun and the
wind?

do you feel particularly blessed by the breeze,
or tanned by the summer's heat?
is your hair always perfectly tousled?
can you walk bare foot without being burned by
the ground?

please, what is it like
to be loved by the gods?

and what is it like to be fought over?

are there ever days when the wind blows clouds
to block out the sun's rays?
are there ever times when the sun cannot warm
you
through the gusting gales?

is it worth it?

is it worth being loved by the gods?

is it worth being loved by the sun and the wind?

i imagine you wouldn't say so.

OCTAVIA THE YOUNGER

Octavia, sister of Emperor Augustus, married Mark Antony. After his death, she took in his four children he had with other women.

you are the most noble of women.
please, do not forget that.

do not let a man like him-
a liar like him,
ruin everything wonderful that you are.

you have always done more than your duty.
even elysium is not worthy of you.

MEDUSA I

out of a thousand villains
in a thousand stories,
you did not deserve this.

you are a victim,
not a criminal,
and I am sorry
you were punished in this way.

ATLAS

it didn't all happen at once.
it happened over days, weeks.

the sky:

that's how we knew.
we knew there was another fallen soldier
amongst the golden blood of the rest.

the sky.

it came down.

he couldn't hold it on his shoulders forever.

the sky fell, and we, underneath it, watched
as the clouds grew closer, inch by inch.

it didn't happen in a second, but slowly.
the sky took its time
falling to the ground.

they were never supposed to meet,

and we were never supposed to know how it felt
to wave our hands through the clouds,
and have them come back wet.

i can still hear the screams of grief.

whether they're for him,
or for us,
i do not know.

PERSEPHONE

Story I:

You were taken,
a flower in your youth,
a dark arm around your waist
dragging you down,
down,
down.

How you screamed,
and your screaming called up to Zeus,
and your screaming brought the cavalry,
and your screaming gave you freedom,
even if it was only half formed.

Story II:

You wandered away from your field,
following the shadow you had glimpsed;
you had never seen darkness like that before.

You fell in love with the curves of architecture,

with the garden of vibrant gem stone fruits,
with a king of inevitability and truth.

Story III:

When you walk away from your flowers,
remember to stop and look around.
Remember to memorise the way the stalks
stretch as they are caressed by the wind,
and the way the petals strain
to touch your fingertips.

When you eat the pomegranate,
only eat half.
Only eat enough to keep you bound
to a man of death for part of the year,
and bound to the world of life for the rest.

Do not be afraid, do not shed a tear.
You were born to be a bridge between life and
death.
Your smiles will light up the dungeons
of the pits of hell,
and when you return,
you'll craft flowers in his image.

HYACINTHUS II

did you ever think you would die this way?

i suppose not.

i imagine that being killed
by the wind –
by a god so in love with you –
was something you never expected.

did you ever think you would live this way?

it was never out of the question.

a beautiful man like you,
with a lovely smile like that –
being chased by the gods
was never off the table.

did you ever think you would come back this
way?

never.

being brought back by the sun
from the blood that dripped to the ground
as wonderful purple flowers
truly must've been surprising.

NARCISSUS I

if i could give you anything,
i would give you the ability to love.
i would tilt your chin away from the surface
of the water,
and show you the world that you've missed.

how you were mourned,
because your love was so narrow.
how your body drooped,
when you couldn't look away.

yes,

i would give you love for others.

i would wind the arms of the clock backwards
and trees would become saplings become seeds.

i would wade into the pool, stand directly over
your reflection
and turn your eyes to something new,
so maybe you could learn to find joy
in something other than your own likeness.

i would hand you love,
and you would be able to share it with someone
else.

but the seeds are becoming saplings becoming
trees,
and when i step away from the water you rush
straight back to it.
your eyes lull only after years
and your body no longer holds itself up

you are the warning painted over the mirrors,
yet you are not disappointed.

why would you be?

in death, we remember you,
and you never wanted to be forgotten.

APOLLO

For some reason, I love you the most.

Don't let it go to your head
(yet it will, of course,)
but I love reckless boys and you
are the king of the uncontrollable.

Indecisiveness burns through
your godly veins,
fusing with the ichor
of the immortals.

You are the god of everything you loved,
even if it had just been for a day.
You mastered every instrument known to man,
and wove poems of pure light.

You drove the sun across the sky,
saw the future when you looked down to man,
and set their broken bones
with a wave of your hand.

You were wild, young one,

(old one, four thousand years under your belt),
you loved fearlessly and eternally,
forgetting how others felt.

Untamed boys like you are to be avoided,
I know this well.
But there's something under that façade
of boyish smirks and bronze skin.

Beneath it all, there is Daphne,
there is Hyacinthus,
and there is a love so powerful
that it still makes your heart tremble.

There is tragedy beneath your halo,
there is torment under your skin.
You have blamed and beaten yourself
for long enough.

All that is left is to forgive.

ECHO

If you need help,
tell me, please.

Please.

You need help?

Help?

I can't find you anywhere.
Are you invisible?

Invisible?

Yes. Invisible.
Cannot be seen.

Cannot be seen.

I know you love him.

Love him.

But can't you see
that he does not care?

Care?

If he cared he would
look away from that
mirror of his. He would
see you standing there.

There.

Yes, I know he's there.
He's always there, by that
reflecting pool he loves so much.
Has he ever looked at you?

You?

No. He hasn't looked at me.
He'll never look at me.
He'll never love me, just like
how he'll never love you.

Never love you.

Yes. Exactly.

Exactly.

So, now you understand,
Will you come away?

Away?

Yes, leave him here,
explore the world,
be your own myth
away from him.

Away from him.

Let's go, come with me.
Yes or no.

No.

No.

No.

Why not?
Why would you stay?

Stay?

I can't stay, not with him.

With him.

Is that how much you love him?

Love him?

That you are willing to stay?

Stay?

He'll never love you back,
you know.

Know.

And you'll always be invisible.

Always be invisible.

I can't believe you're fine with that.

Fine with that.

Really? Are you?
Yes or no.

No.

PERSEUS

How could one borne from golden glitter
have such torment ravaging their bones?
The gods gave you such beautiful gifts
and yet you use them to slice the head
from the shoulders of one who deserves it
no more than you.

A hero amongst men, so is said,
yet still death follows you in your wake,
skin to stone, beating hearts to cement
in a second. You are a king,
Perseus, but a warrior first, a pawn
of the gods and their mistakes.

Slay the monster and save the princess,
marry her and kill the man she was betrothed to.
Murder your father and take the throne.
A man borne from golden glitter;
such a beautiful way to create
an unstoppable soldier.

LIVILLA

Livilla murdered her husband in an attempt to gain power.
A "condemnation of memory" was voted for her, so it's
difficult to identify portraits of her.

A condemnation of memory,
let us forget that you ever existed,
a thorn amongst flowers,
going out of your way to make
the optimistic explorers bleed.

Plots always end in death,
or had you not yet learned from history?
Did you not look back
to see who came before,
who tried before,
who died before?

Oh, young one,
your heart was not pure,
it leaked the poison that you fed
to your lover,
but tasted sweet on your tongue.

NARCISSUS II

In a thousand different stories,
there you sit before your mirror,
your reflective pool of shining water.

In a thousand different stories,
you grow old and sallow,
yet still so beautiful that you cannot
turn away.

In a thousand different stories,
you lean so close to the water
that it fills your lungs when you fall in,
and you drown within your own wonder.

In a thousand different stories,
you stay for so long that your legs
grow roots, and your body becomes a flower,
forever lovely in the echo of the water.

PYTHIA

Pythia was the name given to the High Priestess of Apollo
who was otherwise known as the Oracle of Delphi.

Did you ever see a horror?

Did you ever see a monster so large
that your legs gave way, even though
you knew that it wasn't real –
that it was all a vision amongst the green fog
of Apollo's powers?

Did you ever see the horror;
the beasts and the creatures that crawled
through the dark, and scraped their claws
into the chests of their victims?

Did you ever tell them about it?
The innocent ones who were to face the trials,
who would complete their quests and
wear laurels of victory after being scarred
by their torture?

Did you ever tell them to stop,
to wait, to not go on this one journey?

To not save the damsel, to not kill the beast,
to not walk the maze, fight the war,
do as the gods say?

Did you ever tell the heroes
that they were walking towards their deaths?

No?
Well, you should have.

MASADA

Masada was palace where Jewish zealots took shelter after the Siege of Jerusalem. They decided they would rather kill each other than be slaves to the Roman Empire.

An impenetrable fortress, and yet,
from the inside, you burned.
Fire kills as quickly as a thousand soldiers,
and your bodies disintegrated to ashes,
the slits in your throats hidden
behind the curling of the smoke.

You are murder upon murder upon suicide,
a torch lighting your grave,
flickering yellow across your red,
across your wife's red,
across your child's.

Oh, you rebels, you kings in your palace,
you would rather face the burning
than the chains;
would rather spill your lovers' blood
than hand your soul away.
Oh, you rebels,
you refugees,

you fighters and zealots of a holy cause.

When the soldiers come,
I will not tell them where you are.
When they build their road to your door,
I will not help them knock it down.
But I will not slit the throats of your children,
I will not help you burn.

And you seven, righteous must be your hearts,
if you survived a genocide,
a thousand suicides.
You seven, you children, you women, you innocents,
cry with relief and mourning.

Oh, you seven.
Today, the chains will come to you.
Today, you will see the bodies.
Tomorrow, you will try to forget Masada.
Forever, you never will.

MEDUSA II

Under the light of the stars,
you were taken,
and hurt,
and raped,
and in the morning,
you were punished for it.

Your snakes hiss out of injustice,
and your stare is a spit
at the foot of Athena.

Let Poseidon turn to stone,
let them all harden and become statues.
Your righteous anger will fuel you,
oh gorgon, oh beautiful maiden,
who deserved better than a god
who did not know the meaning of consent.

And when the hero comes to defeat you,
turn him into ashes.
You are a machine of war, now,
and that is not your fault,
but he will only see the monster

you were forced to become –
So slay the hero, and then the gods.

You deserved better than all of them.

HYACINTHUS III

two men came to me the other day,
one with wings and the scent of spring,
a cool breeze following him as if on a leash;
the other like the sun with bronze curls
and a voice the sound of music.

i thought instantly of you,
and i almost wanted to trace your footsteps.

they told me they loved me,
one so handsome and the other so beautiful,
and i so dearly wanted to believe them.

maybe they did love me,
i told them, remorse painted across my face,
but they had loved you, too, once.
and whilst they are free to love and love again,
i cannot come between the wind and the sun,
i cannot fall in love with one but not the other.

the air turned cold and the wind violent,
but still i turned away.
i picked a bouquet of you on the way home,

your pinks and purples so precious in my hands.

it would've been a joy to love the wind,
and an honour to love the sun,
but you had thought the same once,
and it had torn you apart.

DAEDALUS

ICARUS:

You told him not to fly so high, right?
You told him to stay away from the sun,
to not let his wax melt,
to not let himself fall into the ocean,
to drown with the weight of his bronze wings
on his back…
right?

PERDIX:

You pushed him, right?
You watched your nephew's genius
radiate out from his skin;
his intellect so quick and incredible
that you simply couldn't keep up.
It was envy that did it,
right?

DAEDALUS:

You didn't deserve your life, right?

You didn't deserve to live so long,
to create the master of the labyrinth,
to change the world with your ideas.
You know what you did,
you know you deserved your punishments.
You killed them…
right?

SCORPUS

Scorpus was the most famous chariot racer in all of ancient Rome. He won 2048 races before dying at aged 26.

I am Scorpus, and yes my blood runs red
like the clothes that adorn my back.
How would you tell between my loyalties
and my destruction, I will never know.

He is Scorpus and we watch in adoration,
throats hoarse from screaming over the thunder
of the hooves, over the blare of trumpets,
over his beaming smile as he holds the palms of
triumph.

We are Scorpus, us one in the same,
adrenaline that burns through our veins,
and the weight of victory heavy upon our
shoulders.
So heavy that our bones collapse in.

You are Scorpus, cut down by shears.
Atropos never looked from her thread when she
sliced,
and your short years vanished

behind the blades.

Oh, Scorpus, did fate adore you
or abhor the air you breathed?
To give you the wonders of success as you lived,
but to pluck you, a flower in his youth.

ACHILLES II

I beg of you, fight Hector.
Fight him for all that you are worth,
and cut his head off from his body.

I know – I understand, that you
do not wish to fight in a war that is not yours.
You are done being a pawn
in a never-ending chess match
between bitter foes.

But if you do not fight,
he will.
And if he fights,
if he dons your armour and marches
your men into battle.

He will die.

And with him, so will you.

So, please, fight Hector.
Do not become the tragedy you were born to be.

LEGENDS

ABOUT THE AUTHOR

Bethany Nolan was born in 1998 in Hastings, England. She is an avid reader, writer and collector of art supplies she'll never use.

Her ultimate goal is to kick butt in the impending zombie apocalypse, but short of that, would really just like to travel around the world, and have an unlimited supply of money to support her.

This is her first poetry chapbook, and she's very proud of the outcome.

Printed in Great Britain
by Amazon